Original title:
Petals Adrift

Copyright © 2025 Creative Arts Management OÜ
All rights reserved.

Author: Harris Montgomery
ISBN HARDBACK: 978-1-80567-011-7
ISBN PAPERBACK: 978-1-80567-091-9

The Art of Letting Go

A sock took flight, it soared with pride,
Left its mate, they had a ride.
A breeze declared, 'You're free today!'
The laundry laughed, that's how they play.

Through gusts of wind, a sandwich scaled,
On crusts of courage, it had sailed.
With mustard hopes, it paved the way,
And found a feast—now here to stay!

Shadows of Youth

A kite once danced in the blue sky,
Chased by laughter, oh my, oh my!
It flipped and flopped with glee so bold,
While grass stains told of stories old.

A tricycle rolled with squeaky cheer,
Raced through puddles, without a fear.
With ice cream dreams tangled in hair,
Those sunny days, beyond compare.

Meadow Whispers

A butterfly wore a tutu bright,
Twisted and twirled in pure delight.
The daisies giggled in the sun,
Said, 'Join the dance, it looks like fun!'

Bumblebees hummed a silly song,
As they buzzed and bounced all day long.
With nectar sips, they laughed and played,
In fields of joy, worries delayed.

Autumn's Gentle Caress

A squirrel donned a stylish hat,
Critiques were loud, 'What's up with that?'
He scurried forth, not one to care,
Fashion in acorns, beyond compare.

Leaves tumbled down, did a little dance,
Joined the chaos in a frolicsome prance.
With pinecone friends, they rolled along,
Sprinkling laughter, their merry song.

Transient Grace

A flower sneezed, much to its shame,
Its pollen flew, a fragrant game.
Bees giggled, buzzing with delight,
As petals danced into the night.

One tried to twirl, but fell instead,
Landed on a snail, who fled.
"No time for romance, it's not my date!"
The flower laughed—it was just fate!

The sun peeked out, quite a tease,
Daring blooms to catch the breeze.
With each gust, a flower-bound chase,
Frantic racing—a floral race!

So here's to blooms with goofy flair,
Life's too short for perfect hair!
In the garden, chaos reigns,
But joy is found in silly gains.

Remnants of a Fading Day

As shadows stretch and petals yawn,
The bloom brigade prepares for dawn.
They wink at dusk, a lovely tease,
With whispers carried on the breeze.

One bud claims it's too awake,
While others plot a grand mistake.
A midnight snack of dew and light,
With tiny parties 'til first light!

The moon, it laughs, a mischievous sight,
Watching blossoms party all night.
Each dance step clumsy, but who would care?
They twirl and tumble, free as air!

But as the dawn begins to draw,
The blooms all groan, it's such a flaw!
Another day of sun and fun,
Till night returns, then we can run!

Serene Surrender

In a gentle breeze, the petals sigh,
A lazy dance, oh me, oh my!
They float along, with carefree grace,
Like little boats in a flower race.

One took a swim, right in a drink,
Not a good choice, we all did think.
"Help! I'm afloat!" it cried in glee,
"Who knew this tea could set me free?"

Amidst the chaos, friends unite,
Trading stories of their flight.
A sunflower's tale of a bumblebee,
Who mistook it for a hollow tree!

With laughter bright, they share their woes,
Each fall and fumble just adds to prose.
A truce declared, with nectar cheers,
In this flower world, there are no fears!

Echoes of Bloom

As daylight fades, the flowers snicker,
A butterfly winks, oh, how it flickers!
They recall mischief of days gone by,
When one petal soared, though it aimed high.

It landed on a baker's hat,
"I'm a topping! Taste me!" it said, quite brash.
The baker laughed and sent it back,
Yet the bloom just smiled, "I'm on the map!"

The daisies hatched a sneaky plan,
To tickle a cat, a bold span!
Paws flew wildly, flowers in a tangle,
Hilarity grew, in nature's jangle!

At sunset's glow, laughter will ring,
In gardens where silliness takes wing.
With each petal's tale, we find delight,
In echoes of bloom, and a giggle's light.

Dances in the Twilight

Upon the breeze they twirl and spin,
Giggling leaves with mischief within,
A squirrel pranced through a straw hat,
While two birds danced like a friendly spat.

Moonlight paints a floor so bright,
Where shadows join in a silly fight,
A toad serenades with a croak so bold,
As fireflies blink, their stories unfold.

The night wears laughter like a crown,
While frogs in tuxedos take a bow down,
With fluffy clouds acting as chairs,
And the stars tossing candy from their lairs.

So twirl your socks, and don't forget,
The twilight's charm, you won't regret,
Join the hustle of nature's fun,
As night grins wide, her work now done.

Serenade of the Unseen

In the garden, whispers play,
Lively fruits come out to sway,
A carrot jiggles with a wink,
As radishes nod without a blink.

Behind the leaves, a distant cheer,
Tomatoes blushing as friends draw near,
A butterfly with slippery feet,
Practices moves, but can't find a beat.

Lettuce rolls in quirky shows,
With squash doing spins like a pro,
The nightingale croons a cheeky tune,
As the cucumbers start to swoon.

In this hidden, leafy ball,
Everyone's welcome, short and tall,
For once unseen, unite with glee,
A garden's magic for all to see.

Dreams in Blossom

Beneath the blooms, a secret's spun,
Where daisies giggle and have their fun,
A bumblebee dons a top hat wide,
And struts around with ants as his guide.

Tulips compete for a silly crown,
While violets laugh and tumble down,
A dandelion shouts, 'Let's all play!'
And clouds drift by in a fluffy ballet.

Berry bushes share juicy jokes,
As butterflies tease with clever hoaxes,
The sun tickles petals, bright and bold,
Transforming the garden into a show of gold.

So close your eyes in this funny lair,
Where dreams bloom big, with laughter to spare,
In nature's realm, absurd and true,
Each whimsy-coated moment is meant for you.

Shadows of the Heart

In twilight's grip, shadows start to play,
They wiggle like kids who don't want to stay,
A heart-shaped hedge begins to prance,
As laughter spins in a leafy dance.

With giggles echoing through the trees,
A dandelion's wishes float on the breeze,
Moonbeams chase fireflies like old friends,
While cracking jokes on how the night ends.

A raccoon juggles acorns with flair,
While owls debate who has the best hair,
The wind joins in with a gentle hum,
As every shadow knows how to have fun.

So let your heart wander where shadows do sing,
In this playful realm, embrace everything,
For in the whispers of the night's mirth,
Lies a tapestry woven with joy on Earth.

Dancing on Soft Currents

A breeze that tickles like a feather,
It swirls around, a laugh together.
Leaves do the cha-cha, how they sway,
Who knew a gust could steal the day?

With every twist, we leap and twirl,
Float like a dancer in a wild whirl.
Grasshoppers recite the latest beat,
As nature's party's quite the treat.

Caterpillars joining with silly flair,
Butterflies giggle, without a care.
The sun in jest winks through the trees,
And here we are, caught in the breeze.

Laughter echoes through the light,
As colors shimmer, pure delight.
So grab a friend and take a hop,
For springtime frolic will never stop!

Drifting Sentiments of Spring

Blossoms giggle in the sunny's glow,
Tickling bees as they come to and fro.
Each bloom whispers secrets of the day,
While ants march on like they own the play.

Over the hills, they frolic and bound,
Sipping sunlight, spreading cheer all around.
The wind tells jokes to the clouds up high,
While dandelions aim for the sky.

Laughing streams gurgle with delight,
As tadpoles wiggle, oh what a sight!
A joke from a turtle—slow and grand,
Spring is the laughter we all understand.

So join the fun, don't miss the ride,
As life unfolds with joy and pride.
In this season of whims and grins,
New adventures await where laughter begins!

A Voyage of Color and Light

Sailing along on hues of the morn,
Bright pinks and yellows, no reason to mourn.
Clouds wear silly hats made of cream,
As rainbows giggle, it's a dream team.

Twisting and turning on the lake's face,
Ripples are laughing in a playful race.
Fishes leap up, and land with a splash,
While ducks perform a synchronized dash.

Hopping through fields where daisies peek,
Each one grinning, "Come take a sneak!"
The sun is a spotlight, shining on fun,
As colors collide, together they run.

So join this whimsical, vibrant spree,
Life's a riot of colors, wait and see.
With laughter as wind guiding the way,
Let's dance on this boat until the end of the day!

Echoes of a Fragrant Journey

On fragrant breezes, smiles waft around,
With roses telling jokes without a sound.
Lavenders twist, wearing crowns of glee,
While tulips hum sweet tunes, come dance with me.

Buzzy bee chorus tipsy and bright,
Jive with the flowers, oh what a sight!
Each synchronized flutter, a grand ballet,
Who knew plants could party it up this way?

Whiffs of jasmine pull us along,
In this fragrant ballad, we all belong.
The daisies chuckle, softening the air,
Join in the laughter, forget every care.

So let's skip down this aromatic lane,
With giggles and scents, let's entertain.
Life blooms joyfully in each gentle twist,
In this fragrant symphony, we can't resist!

The Tale of Drifted Dew

In the morning glow, the dew did shine,
But a giggling breeze made it unwind.
Rolling off leaves with such a glee,
It danced in circles, wild and free.

Droplets in races, oh what a sight,
Sprinkling laughter, pure delight.
One took a leap, ended in a mug,
Caffeinated chaos, just like a bug.

Grass blades giggled, shifting to see,
How the dew joined jigs, oh so carefree!
"Watch out!" they squeaked, "Here comes the sun!"
With slippery humor, oh what fun!

At the end of the day, they finally lay,
On the ground, grinning after their play.
Nature's pranksters, joyous and bright,
Turning a morn into sheer delight!

Surrendering to the Whispering Breeze

A gentle wind, with a cheeky smile,
Calls the leaves for a playful trial.
"Come dance with me, oh foliage fair,
Let's loop and twirl without a care!"

The flowers giggle, petals a-flutter,
What a comedy, all in a clutter!
With each gust, they tumble and sway,
"Oh dear!" they laugh, "Not again today!"

The trees are chuckling, roots in a bind,
As the breeze teases, leaving them behind.
Catching a ride on a skimming cloud,
"I'm off to the circus!" it shouts, so loud!

As twilight falls with a wink and a tease,
The garden sighs, "Let's all just freeze."
Caught mid-laugh, with nature's mischief,
They dream of winds that'll give them a lift!

A Symphony of Softly Falling Dreams

As the sun dips low, dreams flutter down,
In a symphony wearing night's crown.
Each dream a petal, bright and neat,
Falling like notes, a whimsical beat.

A cow jumped high and chirped like a bird,
While a daisy hummed, just slightly absurd.
Clouds floated by on their fluffy white backs,
Whispering secrets and silly little hacks.

"Oh look!" giggled grass, as dreams took flight,
"Who needs a dreamer when we have the night?"
With each little flop, dreams popped like fizz,
Bringing a chuckle to all that there is.

Finally, moonlight, in laughter, declared,
"Let's gather these dreams; no need to be scared.
Together we'll dance on this starlit stage,
Crafting a tale, written page by page!"

Gossamer Threads of Nature's Caress

In the web of dawn, where shadows play,
Nature weaves stories in bright array.
Silken threads of laughter and cheer,
Tickling the blooms, the bumbles come near.

Spiders celebrate, weaving their tales,
While ants do a conga, raising their tails.
The flowers stifle giggles, share an inside joke,
As a butterfly slips, in a fanciful cloak.

"Oh dear!" whispers grass, "Did you see that?"
As a ladybug spins, all in a spat.
The wind joins the fun, rustling with glee,
Fluffing the feathers of all who can see!

Night brings the curtain on this merry spree,
But whispers of fun softly linger with glee.
In the tender embrace of twilight's caress,
Nature chuckles softly, all her secrets, no less!

Nature's Ebb and Flow

In the garden, grass does jig,
A worm just danced, what a big gig!
Bees wear shades, buzzing so bold,
As daisies gossip, stories unfold.

Raindrops laugh as they slide and splat,
Jumping on leaves, then splashing a cat!
Squirrels protest, their nuts on a spree,
Claiming the ground, "That's our freebie!"

Butterflies flutter, in silly flight,
Chasing each other, what a delight!
But tripping on petals, they whirl and twirl,
Nature's fun circus, in a grand swirl!

With nature's quirks, no one feels low,
Just a laugh fest, watch it all flow!
Life in the wild is odd but bright,
Join in the fun, it feels just right!

Follow the Breeze

A breeze whispered, "Catch me if you can!"
The leaves giggled, doing a fan dance plan.
Dandelions squealed, puffing with flair,
While twigs grumbled, "Hey, that ain't fair!"

Clouds drift by, with a cheeky grin,
Rolling along in a fluffy spin.
The sun peeked out, said it's a game,
While shadows sulked, "I'm always to blame!"

Grass blades chuckled, tickled by toes,
As we ran wild with the playful crows.
A squirrel, a thespian, stole the scene,
Acting out stories of a brave marine!

So, follow the breeze, lose track of time,
Don't mind the mess, it's all in rhyme!
Nature's a jest, teasing our eyes,
Join the ruckus, under bright skies!

Morning's Lost Touch

Morning yawns, scratching its head,
Sunshine stumbles, almost in bed.
Birds drop notes for a sleepy tune,
While coffee beans join the cartoon.

A squirrel in slippers, on a stroll,
Waving hello to a sleepy mole.
Dew drops giggle, slipping off leaves,
"It's too early for mischief, oh please!"

The flowers yawn, stretching so wide,
Winking at bees who can't decide.
Breezes snicker as they float by,
"Let's laugh together, under this sky!"

So join the frolic, don't miss the show,
Mornings are funny, let your joy grow!
With nature's jokes, life's a big clutch,
Embrace the charm, for morning's lost touch!

Kaleidoscope of Transience

Colors swirl in a wondrous spin,
As petals gossip and giggle within.
The sun tickles the leaves, oh so bright,
While shadows play tag, out of pure fright.

Butterflies waltz, doing a jig,
While ladybugs strut, feeling quite big.
A flower sneezes, causing a stir,
Its neighbor chuckles, "What was that blur?"

Clouds change hats, from fluffy to gray,
Dramatic shifts in their playful display.
Rainbows appear, then vanish like dreams,
Laughter echoes, like glimmering beams!

In this swirl of life, funny and bright,
Nature's a stage, a true delight.
So twirl and spin in this lovely dance,
For every moment is pure happenstance!

Serene Melodies of Nature's Kiss

Breezes hum a cheeky tune,
As squirrels dance in afternoon.
With acorns flying through the air,
A nutty fate, they do declare.

Sunbeams tickle blades of grass,
As ants engage in dandy sass.
A flower sneezes, pollen flies,
"Excuse me," it says, with blooming sighs.

Bees buzzing loud, they can't sit still,
Chasing dreams atop a hill.
Bumbling friends in yellow jackets,
Play hide and seek in garden brackets.

Frogs croak jokes along the brook,
Reading leaves like an open book.
Nature sings in giggles sweet,
In this wild and wacky retreat.

Cascading Colors of Distant Shores

Waves play tag, they splash and roar,
Surfboards flying, tumble on shore.
Seagulls cackle, sharing the bait,
While crabs march in a soldier's gait.

A sunset painted with strokes of glee,
Yellows and reds, a sight to see.
Jellyfish float, they dance with flair,
Throwing a party in salty air.

Beach umbrellas, like daisies on sand,
Wobble and sway, can't quite stand.
Children's laughter fills the sea,
As sandcastles fall, oh what a spree!

In a treasure hunt, X marks the spot,
But here comes a dog—oh boy, what a plot!
With a muddy paw, it digs in deep,
Finding treasures—a tasty treat!

The Sky-Bound Reverie of Spring

Clouds have giggles like ballooned cats,
Dancing softly upon their mats.
A kite takes off, a raucous cheer,
Until it wraps around a deer!

Sunshine beams in a playful race,
While flowers bloom with silly grace.
Dandelions blow like wishes bright,
Who knew they could take flight at night?

Bumbles buzz with hats on heads,
Mocking sparrows, forming threads.
As laughter rings through fields aglow,
Little antics put on quite a show.

A robin's song, off-key but bold,
Turns the routine into pure gold.
Nature's orchestra, flawed but true,
Makes even springtime bloom anew.

Flutters of Life on Gentle Streams

Butterflies sip on sweet tea leaves,
While dragonflies tease with autumn weaves.
A turtle paddles, slow and fair,
Chasing fish with a curious stare.

Leaves drift down from lofty heights,
Like waltzing dancers in soft twilight.
A frog jumps 'round, a grand brigade,
"Catch me if you can!" it loudly played.

Crickets chirp their late-night song,
In a rhythm that feels so wrong.
But the fireflies twinkle in delight,
Flickering jokes in the cool of night.

With every ripple, laughter flows,
Creating music only nature knows.
In this wild, whimsical stream so bright,
Life flutters on, a comical flight.

The Scented Voyage of Time

A time machine made of daisies,
Drifting on trails of sunny breezes.
Each second smells like raspberry pie,
Tick-tock giggles, oh my, oh my!

Toasters toast as clocks tick by,
Butterflies in raincoats, oh so spry.
A sandwich race, who'll win the fight?
The jam-packed laughs bring sheer delight!

Jellybeans scattered on the floor,
Dancing squirrels knock at the door.
With every flip, we laugh and glide,
Time's funny jokes can't be denied!

In this garden where time can play,
We leap and bounce through the bouquet.
Laughter's the key, our hearts ignite,
On this fragrant trip, everything feels right!

Soft Silhouettes Against the Sky

Kites made of socks are zooming high,
As dancing bunnies wave goodbye.
Pigs in tutus frolic with flair,
While giraffes play hopscotch in midair.

Clouds turn purple, and llamas cheer,
Twirling hats and giggling near.
A squirrel in shades with style so bright,
Sips lemonade while taking flight.

In this world where shadows tease,
Ticklish breezes swirl with ease.
We chase the sun, and oh, what a sight,
Soft shapes spinning in pure delight!

So grab your friends and take a ride,
On this rooftop where dreams collide.
Every whimsy makes the heart sigh,
In soft silhouettes against the sky!

Fluttering Dreams in a Sunlit Glade

In a sunlit glade where dreams take wing,
A chorus of giggles begins to sing.
Marshmallow clouds with candy canes,
Sprinkle laughter like gentle rains.

Dancing shoes with squeaky tunes,
Join the party with singing raccoons.
'A bubble parade floats through the trees,
With flippy-floppy hats zooming in the breeze.

Bumblebees don tuxedos to prance,
While ladybugs waltz in a dainty dance.
Here, giggles bounce like a bright spring breeze,
Life's a canvas, and laughter's the tease!

So lie in the grass and watch them play,
With fluttering dreams that whisk you away.
In this sunlit glade, feel joy ignite,
As silly moments take flight tonight!

Meadow's Embrace in Serene Flight

A pillow fight with fluffy sheep,
As giggles rise, not a soul's asleep.
Grass tickles toes like a feathered tease,
While daisies giggle in the warm breeze.

In this meadow where fun's the plan,
An octopus stitches a colorful band.
Jumping jacks with squirrels in suits,
A royal tea with fruity roots!

Kites shaped like fish begin to soar,
As rabbits play chess on the forest floor.
With every stroke, colors unite,
In the meadow's embrace, oh what a sight!

So chase the sun and twirl with glee,
Let your laughter set you free.
In this whimsical place, we take flight,
Finding joy where everything feels right!

Flight of the Free Spirit

In the breeze, they twirl and sway,
Bumping into folks like it's play.
A dance-off with the morning light,
Laughing, bouncing, such a sight!

They hitch a ride on grandma's hat,
Whispering secrets, oh, how they chat!
With a giggle, they escape the ground,
Chasing the birds with zeal profound.

Giggling softly in the warm sunbeam,
Creating an unpredictable dream.
Unexpected guests at a picnic feast,
Making wisecracks, it's no time to cease!

While dancing amid the skies so blue,
They've decided to join a cha-cha crew.
With every flutter, a fanciful prank,
Leaving smiles with each little prank!

Hues of Goodbye

Colors cascade in a playful swirl,
As goodbyes giggle and twirl.
Yellow and pink with a wink so bright,
Twirling away into the night.

Oh, how they play with the evening air,
Spilling laughter everywhere!
Tossing hues like confetti high,
As if aiming for the giant pie!

With a splash of orange, a dash of green,
They're re-choreographing the scene.
Dancing hearts, so bold and spry,
Their canvas holds a chuckle or sigh.

At the end, when daylight fades,
They send kitschy serenades.
Goodbyes that burst like funny jokes,
Sending off the wayward folks!

Songs of the Seasons

Each season sings a quirky tune,
Like squirrels dancing to the moon.
Winter whispers, slip and slide,
While summer grins in a sunny stride.

Spring's a jester, tossing blooms,
Taunting bees in fuzzy costumes.
Autumn laughs with a rustle and cheer,
As leaves join in on a grand ordeal!

Seasons trade their silly hats,
Chasing each other like friendly cats.
With every shift, a chuckle flies,
As nature shares her punchline ties.

The songs blend in a wondrous way,
Like children laughing in ballet.
So let's join in the merry blend,
With giggles that never seem to end!

Unfolding Horizons

Horizons stretch with a playful wink,
As if to say, 'Come on, think!'
They unfold like a treasure map,
Inviting all for a fun little yap.

Mischief lurks in the dawn's embrace,
Chasing shadows with a happy face.
Colors peel back, revealing the game,
Each stretch a giggle, never the same.

With a flutter of wings, they tease and sway,
Unfolding dreams that refuse to stay.
Every sunset drops a funny quip,
Leaving the stars in a comic script.

Here at the edge, laughter flows wide,
On the road, we skip and slide.
With each horizon, a joke takes flight,
We're the punchline in the night!

Threads of Existence

Life is a tapestry, they say,
But mine's more of a fray.
My socks never find a match,
And my plans? Just a scratch!

I trip on the strings I create,
Like a jester, I contemplate.
Each knot holds a chuckle or two,
As I weave through the wild and the blue.

That time I lost my last stitch,
Was it fate or a glitch?
With threads of laughter, I bind,
The chaos that I call my mind.

In the loom of my daily plight,
I tumble and twirl in delight.
Though tangled, I dance and I spin,
For what's life without some whim?

Reveries in Flight

I dream of wings made of cheese,
Floating high on a breeze.
Mice join me, all chirpy and bright,
We're soaring just out of sight!

With every flap, a giggle escapes,
We dodge the clouds that shape-shift into grapes.
Alas! A pizza slice calls, oh so grand,
We'll hover our way to a cheesy land!

Down below the earth points and laughs,
As I stumble through caloric gaffe.
But in this dream, I can't get enough,
I wear my pizza wings—it's all pure fluff!

And when I wake, it's back to the grind,
With thoughts of cheese still nicely entwined.
Yet every day in this wacky flight,
I'll savor the dreams that feel just right!

Memories Carried by Stardust

My memories dance like sparkles above,
Each twinkling thought is a treasure trove.
I once lost a shoe in a cosmic swirl,
Now I flash my toes to the universe's whirl!

Through the galaxy, my stories parade,
Like a comet with a lemonade.
I stumble on stars, laughing, oops!
My heart floats up like helium loops!

In the void, I misplace my keys,
Even stardust giggles, if you please.
It's cosmic chaos; it's all in the fun,
As I chase my thoughts, a wild cosmic run!

So here's to the twinkling astral delight,
Where every lost memory takes flight.
A shimmer of laughter, a sprinkle of cheer,
I gather my dreams, with joy I steer!

Elysian Wanders

I wandered through fields of marshmallow fluff,
Hopping with bunnies, oh how fun is this stuff!
They snicker and giggle, all in a race,
As they whisk off with a bounce, leaving no trace!

In the land of lost jellies and cream,
I stumbled on cupcakes, a sugary dream.
Frosting rivers, oh what a scene,
Where every sugar rush feels like a queen!

With gumdrop clouds floating up in the air,
I reach for a rainbow, a sight so rare.
But the Giggle-Wind whistles and tickles my nose,
I tumble and tumble, oh where does it go?

Through Elysian fields, the laughter runs wild,
Walking on sunshine, I'm a sugar-fueled child.
And as twilight draws close, I'll wear my bright grin,
For every whimsical wander, I always win!

Breaths of Change

A breeze that tickles, noses flare,
Leaves tumble down without a care.
I chase a leaf, it zooms away,
Who knew a twig could lead astray?

The squirrel steals my very snack,
He grins and scurries down the track.
I shout, 'Hey, that's my lunch you thief!'
But he just chirps in disbelief.

Clouds roll in to play their part,
A burst of rain, oh what a start!
Umbrellas flip, a dance of doom,
Who knew this day would end in gloom?

Yet laughter bubbles, bright and bold,
In strangers' eyes, stories unfold.
We all fall down, we laugh and cheer,
Breaths of change bring joy, my dear.

The Carousel of Time

Round and round, the clock it swings,
Where is the time for fun-filled things?
I hop on a horse that's seen better days,
Its manes are frizzy, it clanks and sways.

Friends spin on chairs, eyes full of glee,
While I hold tight, 'don't lose me!'
A tumble here, a giggle there,
Who knew time had such a flair?

A dance of shadows, swirling bright,
As moments blur in borrowed light.
Tick-tock, tick-tock, the laughter keeps,
Time's a prankster; it never sleeps.

Yet in the chaos, we find our rhyme,
A carousel ride with no end to time.
We twirl and laugh in this wild spree,
Forever young, just you and me.

A Symphony of Softness

A fluffy cloud drifts overhead,
Whispers of laughter, dreams unsaid.
Bouncing rabbits play a tune,
In a meadow, under the moon.

Tickled by petals, soft and light,
Butterflies join, a hilarious flight.
They dance like they've taken a sip,
Of nectar sweet, on a saucy trip.

A bunny hops and slips, oh dear!
His buddy giggles, 'You're no reindeer!'
Puffs of fluff and joyful sound,
This silly symphony knows no bound.

So let's forget our woes today,
And celebrate in a quirky way.
With laughter ringing, we'll softly sway,
In a symphony, come what may.

Faint Traces in the Sunlight

Sunbeams teasing, shadows play,
Chasing giggles, come what may.
A glimmer here, a wink from there,
Footprints scatter with nary a care.

Bees and butterflies, oh what a mix,
Making a ruckus, pulling their tricks.
They buzz and flit in a grand ballet,
In the sunlight, they laugh and sway.

I trip on grass, land in a heap,
With faint traces of laughter to keep.
A dog runs by, pulling his owner,
'Faster, faster!'—what a performer!

As day fades soft, our jokes reset,
With every giggle, we won't forget.
Faint traces linger, like summer delights,
In the golden glow of fading lights.

Whirlwind of Seasons

A leaf took flight in a gusty breeze,
Danced with squirrels, oh what a tease!
It spun through the air, quite a sight,
Waving at folks, with sheer delight.

A raindrop rolled down a window pane,
Joined a race with clouds, feeling quite vain.
But as it slipped, it let out a cheer,
Splashing on rooftops, without any fear.

Winter's snow turned to puddles so slick,
And slipped on his cousin, the old tree stick.
They laughed as they tumbled into the street,
The embrace was cold, but oh, so sweet!

With every season, more games to unfold,
Nature's own circus, a sight to behold.
They frolic and play, in their jolly domain,
Each twist of the wind, a whimsical train.

Unraveled Beauty

A flower once prim, lost her marigold crown,
Complained to a bug, who chuckled, then frowned.
"You're lovely still, with your lopsided grin,
Just let out a giggle, and beauty will win!"

The petals fell off, how could this be fair?
She danced with the dirt, embracing despair.
With each little twirl, a buzz started low,
"You're funnier now, let your wild side show!"

The bee brought some pollen, they started a trend,
The corners of gardens began to extend.
"We're all a bit quirky; it's beauty, not pride!
Embrace your odd edges, let your charm be your guide!"

As colors mismatched, with laughter they grew,
Rejected the rules, made their own rendezvous.
In their sweet rebellion, they flourished with glee,
Unraveled in joy, not what they should be.

Withering Yet Free

A dandelion puff, all fluffy and round,
Blown off the path, to the laughter it found.
"Goodbye to the garden! I'm off to explore,
Life's better in chaos, who's keeping score?"

With threads shed by time, took flight on the breeze,
Said hi to a duck, who was dodging the tease.
"You're whisked from your stem; isn't that just a hoot?
I only waddle on, but you've found a new route!"

A tumbleweed chuckled, rolled past with delight,
"A wanderer now, you were once quite a sight!
Withering may seem like an end to the fun,
But freedom awaits, in the warmth of the sun!"

Together they spun, a whimsical crew,
Embracing the wild, as the fresh morning dew.
With laughter in tow, they danced under skies,
Withering yet free, what a sweet surprise!

Secrets Beneath the Surface

In a muddy bog, where the frogs loved to croak,
Lived a shy lilypad, who just couldn't poke.
"I'm pretty sure I'm just an awkward-green plate,
Silly little lily, my fate's looking great!"

One day a fish with a glimmering tail,
Swam by with a grin, and told quite a tale.
"You may be stuck here, but don't be aghast,
There's wonder down below; let go of the past!"

Curiosity sparked, she took a big leap,
Dove down in the depths, where secrets don't sleep.
Among bubbles and giggles, she found her new crew,
A dance party blooming with water so blue!

Now they swirl and they splash, under ripples of light,
Silly secrets shared, oh what a delight!
The once-shy lilypad, now queen of the scene,
With frogs, and with fish, she reigns evergreen!

The Ballet of Wandering Flora

In the garden, blooms take flight,
Dancing leaves in pure delight.
A daisy twirls, a rose can't sing,
But oh! It knows how to do the fling.

The tulips laugh, they slip and slide,
When breezes pull them, they can't hide.
Their petals swirl, like skirts in spins,
Every turn, the laughter begins.

Daffodils trip on their sunny heads,
While pansies giggle, turning reds.
They form a line, a floral parade,
But watch out, or you might cascade!

As the wind plays tricks, they play back,
Twisting and turning, in a colorful pack.
With each bloomin' step, all worries drift,
In this funny dance, the garden's gift.

Fragments of Color in the Breeze

A butterfly chuckles, painting the air,
While marigolds gossip over there.
The wind tickles tulips, they giggle and sway,
As petals chatter in a bright bouquet.

Zinnias boast with their bright, bold hues,
Saying, "We're here, we refuse to lose!"
The breeze, a prankster, swirls them around,
In a vibrant cha-cha, they all abound.

Dandelions throw wishes, aiming for dreams,
While violets scheme, bursting at seams.
"Oh dear!" says a flower, "I'm having a blast!
But hold on tight, we're spinning so fast!"

As colors collide, laughter erupts,
Nature's own jesters, with petals abrupt.
In this garden realm, joy sets the tone,
With whispers and chuckles, they've happily grown.

A Journey Touched by Sunlit Rain

Raindrops giggle on leafy hats,
While pansies dance with the pitter-pats.
They slip and slide, with a splash and a spin,
In this sun-kissed journey, fun fills their grin.

Petunia prances in puddles galore,
While daisies wink, saying, "Let's explore!"
The sun peeks out, warming their feet,
They hop in time to a funky beat.

With every droplet, their spirits soar,
A floral adventure, who could ask for more?
Bright colors shimmer, like laughter unfurled,
In this wet waltz, they twirl all around the world.

The clouds chuckle softly, covering the sun,
As blossoms rejoice, their journey's begun.
Through sunlit rain, with a skip and a sway,
Their whimsical trek is the best kind of play.

Whimsy of the Blossom Winds

Beneath the sky, the blooms conspire,
To ride the wind, their fun is dire.
A gust comes by, and off they flee,
Spreading laughter, wild and free.

Petals whirl, forming a kite,
While violets giggle at their own flight.
They twist and twirl, like dancers in glee,
"Oh look at us! We're a sight to see!"

Dandelions puff, in a fluffy parade,
"Catch us if you can!" they're not afraid.
The breeze just laughs, pushing them hither,
With silly games, how could they quiver?

As colors collide, happiness blooms,
In this wacky journey, there's no room for glooms.
So let the winds whistle, let the flowers sway,
For in this fun dance, they'll forever play.

A Tapestry of Ephemera

In a garden where daisies dance,
A bee tripped over his polka pants.
He swore he'd twirl and make a scheme,
But stumbled right into a buttercup dream.

Oh, how the roses rolled with glee,
While tulips chuckled atop a spree.
Each flower giggled, petals ablaze,
As bees buzzed off on a silly craze.

The lilies plotted with mischievous sighs,
Planning a prank that would split up the skies.
When the sun came out, they threw a great party,
But the violet got stuck, feeling quite hearty!

So here we thrive in our fragrant fable,
With laughter tangled as we are able.
In a tapestry woven with pollen and laughs,
Join us under the blooms, for whimsical paths.

Lament of the Blooms

Oh, the lilies cried with a wink and a nudge,
They sneakily plotted, they wouldn't budge.
The tulips declared in a voice quite absurd,
"Why fret about winter, it's really quite blurred!"

The roses burst forth in a mock-sob of cheer,
"Another spring passed, oh how we kvetch here!"
While dandelions giggled, lit up like a torch,
"Next season's our time, we'll frolic, of course!"

A daisies' discussion of who's got the best,
Led to a riot, a colorful quest.
As colors collided in a wild ballet,
Who knew blooms could jest in such a bouquet?

So, the blooms lament with laughter, not tears,
As petals playtag through all of the years.
In their garden of shimmering shade,
The chorus of color will never quite fade.

Ghosts of Color

In the twilight, where the shadows blend,
The flowers danced, as if on a trend.
With colors whispering from night's gentle breath,
They plotted joy, conquering death!

A ghost of a daffodil led the troupe,
With a sneaky giggle, they formed a loop.
The lavender moaned, now whispers of lore,
"Did you hear who's asking for flowers galore?"

The marigolds snickered, their petals so bright,
"We haunt all gardens from morning to night!"
They giggled and swayed, weaving tales so grand,
While the moon lit their pranks with a shimmered hand.

So come, join this gathering, where laughter prevails,
With ghosts of the blooms spinning comical tales.
In the garden of giggles, where colors unite,
These cheeky apparitions bring joy to the night.

Silent Gardens

In quiet corners where giggles sprout,
The flowers conspired, there's no doubt.
A sunflower whispered, all sunshine and glee,
"Let's throw a bash, just you and me!"

The peonies blushed, they knew what to do,
They crafted a plan, oh what a crew!
With petals like confetti and laughter in air,
They prepped for a party with flair to spare.

The violets chuckled, "We'll sneak out at dark,
And dance underneath the old willow's arc."
As twinkle lights glimmered on every stem,
The silence was broken by their floral gem.

Thus, in silent gardens, the blooms found their groove,
With rhythm and laughter, they mastered the move.
And when dawn broke, their secrets to keep,
They swayed with a grin, now nestled in sleep.

Soft Echoes of Eternity

A flower sneezed, a petal flew,
Twisting, turning, what a view!
It tickled bees, gave them a fright,
Buzzing round, they took to flight.

The sun looked down, a grin so wide,
"Did you see that?" it tried to hide!
But clouds just giggled, fluffy and bright,
As blossoms danced in sheer delight.

A breeze passed by, a playful tease,
Made every blossom sway with ease.
They spun and twirled, a floral dance,
While ants marched on, lost in a trance.

In laughter's bloom, the garden sighed,
In every corner, joy did glide.
So let us frolic, you and I,
Where petals laugh and never die.

Chasing Shadows

A shadow quick, a game of tag,
With daisies daring, never a drag.
"Catch me if you can!" the petals cried,
As dandelions joined the wild ride.

A snail peeked out, quite bemused,
"You call that fast? You're all confused!"
But the shadows laughed, flickering light,
While flowers bloomed, oh what a sight!

A tulip tripped, went tumbling down,
While sunflowers hooted, the gossip crown.
With every slip, a chuckle grew,
In this wild chase, nothing felt blue.

So let the shadows play their game,
As blooms and giggles ignite the flame.
In burbles of green and colors bright,
Chasing shadows feels just right.

The Path of Forgotten Blooms

In the corner of a garden tucked,
Lay old daisies, a tad bit plucked.
They whispered tales of the wind so spry,
And how butterflies forget to fly.

A weed laughed loud, with glee and zest,
"You old-timers sure need a rest!"
But roses chimed in with sweet replies,
"We've seen it all, oh, don't you cry!"

The mushrooms danced, with hats so wide,
While chickens clucked, their feathers fried.
In this garden, oddities bloom,
A place where flowers embrace their gloom.

Yet as the moon rose, all became bright,
The forgotten ones shone with delight.
For every bloom, old tales retold,
In this patch of laughter, pure and bold.

A Canvas of Change

Once a green field, now a mess,
With paint splattered everywhere, oh yes!
A llama laughed with a brush in hand,
While flowers giggled at his command.

They dipped their heads in colors jive,
Squeezed out laughs, making vibes thrive.
"I want to be blue!" said a rose with glee,
"And I'll be polka-dot!" sang a tiny pea.

So the daisies donned shades of gold,
While tulips turned pink and bold.
The canvas shifted, a merry play,
In this wild garden, colors sway.

Every brush stroke, a chuckle loud,
As nature donned her vibrant shroud.
For in this canvas, change is fun,
Art of the blossoms, second to none.

Driftwood Dreams

A log on the shore, so wise and so bold,
It tells us stories of treasures untold.
Dancing with seagulls, it's found a new way,
To surf through the tides, come join in the play!

With flip-flops in hand, and a smile on my face,
I ride on the waves, it's a whimsical race.
The driftwood just chuckles, a real jokester's glee,
As I tumble and stumble, quite clumsily free!

The sun sets like butter, a golden delight,
The driftwood keeps laughing, oh what a sight!
In dreams made of drift and a splash of the sea,
I'll never stop chasing this wild jubilee!

So here's to the logs that float through the foam,
May every new journey feel just like home.
With giggles and splashes, let's ride till it's night,
And laugh at our folly under the moonlight!

Blossoms on a Breeze

A flower forgot, flew high on the wind,
A giggle of petals, together they twinned.
With pollen for parachutes, off they would soar,
Landing on noses, making people roar!

In gardens they tumble, all pink and quite proud,
Holding a summit, a floral parade loud.
They whispered a secret, oh what would it be?
'Watch out for the bees, they come to make tea!'

The daisies exchanged jokes, while hyacinths sang,
A chorus of colors, what a joyous tang!
With each little gust, they spun 'round like tops,
A jolly ballet till all of them flop!

So raise up your glasses, for flowers so spry,
They brighten our days, oh my, oh my!
A breeze full of laughter, how splendid, indeed,
Life's frivolous blossoms, the heart's only need!

Fragments of Spring

A squirrel named Nutty thought spring was a feast,
He gathered up acorns, a marvelous beast.
But flowers were blooming, oh what a surprise,
He mistook them for muffins, right there before his eyes!

He nibbled and munched with great gusto and cheer,
While petals dropped gently, they'd flutter and veer.
With crumbs on his whiskers, he looked quite absurd,
He laughed at his folly, not thinking it weird!

The daisies applauded, their heads bobbing low,
'Hey Nutty, don't snack on what's meant for a show!'
He promised to stop, but his tummy had dreams,
Of sweet-scented pastries in sunbeam-filled streams.

So here's to the critters who twist and who twirl,
In gardens of spring where their antics unfurl.
A dance of oblivion, of humor and glee,
Where every small blunder is a whimsical spree!

The Dance of Fluttering Leaves

Once leaves had a party, oh what a grand sight,
They twirled and they twinkled, brought joy to the night.
With acorns as guests and squirrels all around,
They danced in the moonlight, a rustling sound.

The wind played the DJ, with tunes oh so bright,
And each little leaf had a fling with delight.
A cascade of laughter, as branches swayed free,
Invisible friendships were danced joyfully!

But soon in their revel, they felt a slight chill,
Their parties were fleeting, so they gathered at will.
'Let's twirl till we drop, before winter arrives!'
They cheered, twirling faster, feeling so alive!

So wave your goodbyes to those leaves on the breeze,
As they twinkle and giggle, and twist with such ease.
A dance of delight as they flutter and weave,
In the tapestry of nature, in colors they leave!

Revelations in Ruins

In the garden of lost socks,\nGnomes play poker at dawn,\nPlants gossip about the rocks,\nWhile squirrels hoard tales till they yawn.\n\nA rubber duck floats in a breeze,\nOutwitting the owls in a match,\nBumblebees dance with such ease,\nWhile jellybeans roll, and we catch.\n\nSunflowers wear hats far too big,\nDandelions start a singing spree,\nWorms breakdance, oh what a gig!\nThe laughter is wild and so free.\n\nAs the wind whispers secrets unheard,\nRainbows nudge clouds for advice,\nLife's silly, if often absurd,\nJust remember to smile, it's nice!

Journeys Yet Unwritten

A snail packs his tiny suitcase,\nWith dreams of the moonlit shore,\nHiccups from lemony embrace,\nWhile crickets debate the score.\n\nFrog leaps high with a trumpet's tune,\nDancing to his own thunder,\nSassier than a raccoon,\nBut stumbles — oh what a blunder!\n\nClouds argue about colors to wear,\nWhile the sun snoozes in a chair,\nFluffy sheep just don't care,\nThey're plotting to prank a bear!\n\nChasing tails through fields of quirks,\nThe world spins on in delight,\nWith every giggle that lurks,\nAdventure awaits, feather-light!

Threads of Time

Clocks laugh as they walk in a line,\nThey tick and they tock with a grin,\nFinding fashion in every design,\nWhile cats plot a paper boat win.\n\nA wise old turtle plays chess,\nWith a crow who won't take a break,\nEach move ends in silliness,\nCreating a laugh with each quake.\n\nTwilight introduces a dance,\nWhere shadows trip over their feet,\nA comet joins in for a chance,\nTo show some moves that are sweet.\n\nTime giggles, it rolls on the floor,\nWith every second — we chuckle,\nLife's an odd pair, for sure,\nSo let's embrace the fun and buckle!

In the land of dancing spoons,\nChopsticks laugh with a pun,\nWhile teacups hum silly tunes,\nAnd coffee drips just for fun.\n\nPancakes fly from grill high,\nLanding lands softly on plates,\nMuffins in a shy pie,\nCompete for the best breakfast rates.\n\nCookies stumble in a race,\nThey tickle the milk in glee,\nEvery bite is a sweet embrace,\nAs crumbs laugh and fly free.\n\nIn a kitchen where chaos create,\nWe feast, as the cat takes a nap,\nSurreal is the joy of our plate,\nLet's savor this delicious trap!

Time's Gentle Brush

In the garden where time plays,
Dandelions dance on sunny rays.
They wiggle and jiggle, without a care,
Next to a snail in a polka-dot chair.

The clock ticks slow, yet I can't be late,
A bee buzzing by, declaring a date.
With laughter that bubbles, we all shall meet,
For lunch with a worm, how quite the treat!

Time sips its tea, oh what a game,
Spinach may shout, but broccoli's tame.
As vegetables giggle, and flowers do sway,
We'll feast on our dreams till the end of the day.

So here's to the fun, where the minutes go wild,
In a world where each hour is lovingly styled.
Let's twirl in this dance that we cannot resist,
And giggle along in a whimsical twist.

A Mosaic of Echoes

The leaves they whisper, secrets on wind,
Do trees gossip too? Oh, where have they been?
With squirrels holding court, on branches they chatter,
Debating the merits of nutty old matter.

A rabbit hops by, with a wink and a smile,
He's off to the races, just sprinting a mile.
The sun beams brightly, greeting each whim,
While shadows play tag; oh, isn't it grim?

In this puzzling patchwork of delight and surprise,
The world is a jigsaw that tickles the eyes.
With each little quirk and each quirky little twist,
We laugh loud and clear, in this sweet, mad abyss.

So gather, oh friends, for the stories we weave,
Of dancing and prancing, in bright autumn leaves.
With echoes of joy hanging thick in the air,
Let's mosaic our laughter, for moments we share.

Fleeting Moments

A butterfly flits, oh what a tease,
It tickles the nose of a snoozing bee.
With each little flutter, the day feels so bright,
It giggles at shadows, a wondrous sight.

The sun winks down at the lazy old cat,
Who stretches and yawns, barely moves an inch flat.
A playful breeze tugs at his fluffy old tail,
While he dreams of fish and a deep, frothy ale.

Oh laugh with me now at the fleeting delight,
In moments so silly, we take to new heights.
With blink-and-you-miss-it shenanigans here,
Let's toast to the chuckles that bring us good cheer!

As laughter rushes, let's savor the fun,
With sprinkles of joy that shine like the sun.
For fleeting are moments, but memories last,
In the quilt of our lives, stitched up from the past.

Timeless Whispers

In the realm of the goofy, where giggles abound,
A frog wears a crown, at the bog he is found.
With a song on his lips and a hop in his step,
He champions the notion that laughter's adept.

Old owls tell tales, but can't finish a line,
For every third thought is a hiccup divine.
They squint through the branches, looking so wise,
Yet trip on their beaks, oh, what a surprise!

The clouds float on by with a chuckle or two,
As they change their shapes, then they rain down on you.
With splashes of smiles that sparkle and spray,
We splash in puddles, come what may.

So gather your giggles, hold them up high,
For timeless the whispers that flutter and fly.
With hearts light as feathers, let's leap and let roam,
In this silly old world, we have found our sweet home.

Beyond the Garden Gate

Past the gate where the wild things grow,
A chicken in boots says, "Don't be too slow!"
She struts and she clucks, in a fashionable gait,
While the rooster proclaims that he's rather first-rate.

The hedgehogs have formed a dance crew beneath,
With prancing and flailing, oh what a sheath!
While snails form a line, for the best seat in town,
To witness the antics of the farmyard clowns.

On the fence, a wise tortoise grins with delight,
As butterflies shimmer in colorful flight.
They share all the gossip, the joy and the fate,
Of charming odd dreams just past the old gate.

So come one, come all to this hilarious show,
Where laughter spills freely, and friendships will grow.
Together we'll wander, through laughter and cheer,
In the land just outside where the fun is so near!

Wandering Memories

In the breeze, old jokes float high,
Each giggle a leaf, oh me, oh my.
Faded laughter dances in the sun,
Who knew memories could be so fun?

A flip-flop flings, then hits a tree,
Wandering tales of you and me.
Chasing echoes, we run, we slide,
Reliving moments, oh, what a ride!

Secrets in the Air

Whispers sprinkled like candy dust,
Every secret swirls—oh, how we trust!
Giggling gnomes share tales of old,
In this silly wind, mischievous and bold.

Balloons drift far, waving goodbye,
Wondering if they'll return to the sky.
Silly stories tumble and glide,
On this jolly breeze, let's take a ride!

Cascading Colors

When pink and yellow start to mix,
Why do rainbows play silly tricks?
Frolicking hues in a vibrant spree,
Making even clouds dance with glee.

Glittery greens in a taffy swirl,
Nature's palette begins to twirl.
Each color shouts, 'Come join the fun!'
In the land where whimsy has just begun.

The Journey of Fragrance

A whiff of cookies drifts from afar,
Chasing scents like a twinkling star.
Sneaky spices, they come to play,
Turning our noses into ballet!

Petunias whisper, 'What's that you smell?'
Lavender laughs, 'Oh, it's a spell!'
Every breeze is a joyful quest,
In this fragrant world, we jest and jest!

The Chase of Light

Bouncing beams on grassy floors,
This game is fun, my feet want more.
I chase the sun, it dances away,
Like a cat with a mouse, come play!

Around the trees, I zig and zag,
Yet it teases, I hear it brag.
"Catch me quick!" it shouts with glee,
Oh, to possess that fleeting spree!

Rolling in laughter, I twist and spin,
Thought I had it, but here comes the wind!
With every step, it slips, it dives,
A game we play where light survives.

In the end, I rest and sigh,
Though I was quick, the sun flies high.
But who needs it, when shadows play?
I'll laugh at night; it's my breakaway!

Nature's Ephemeral Gift

Tiny blooms, bright as a wink,
They tease my nose, they make me think.
"Pick me up!" they shout in glee,
But soon they'll fade, as quick as me!

Daisies dance on the breeze so light,
I start a fight; I'm ready to bite!
A bumblebee buzzes, "This is my turf!"
I giggle and run, not knowing my worth!

Oh fleeting friend, I long to keep,
But they don't care, they just like to leap.
With colors swirling like ice cream spritz,
They vanish, leaving me in fits!

So here we go, a game of chase,
I'll nab a flower, I'll win this race!
But as they giggle and twist away,
I chuckle and dream of my bouquet.

Liquid Colors

Splashes of blue on my old canvas,
Each stroke a smile that feels quite famished.
With orange and green, I create a mess,
My masterpiece now oh-so-stressed!

Drip, drop, the colors flow and mix,
My fingers dance, oh how they flick!
A rainbow fate, nosedive delight,
Who knew art could be such a sight?

Splatters everywhere, the floor is alive,
"Hey, look at me!" I hear colors jive.
But Mom walks in and gasps like she's seen
A rave gone bonkers, a wild cuisine!

With laughter bubbling, she helps me clean,
"Next time, kiddo, be less of a fiend!"
So we brush and splash until it's bright,
Creating our world, a liquid delight!

Surrender to the Current

Floating downstream on a bright pink duck,
Giggles abound, oh what silly luck!
The current tugs, but I wiggle and squirm,
A ride so wild, it makes my head churn!

Waves splash my face, the trees they mock,
I ride like a ship, or perhaps a rock.
With fish in the stream, they wink and dart,
"Join us!" they call, oh what a smart!

A game of tag in nature's embrace,
I wave to the turtle, it's a fun face!
But oops! I hit a log, what a blunder,
My pink duck flips, oh, what a wonder!

Yet with frothy laughter, I find my way,
Faces afloat, we dance and sway.
So here in the stream, with giggles and fun,
I surrender to joy, for the day is begun!

The Lightness of Being

I danced on a breeze, oh what a delight,
My socks mismatched, a comical sight.
In shoes made for storms, I twirled and I spun,
With each wobbly step, I laughed, oh what fun!

A dog in a tutu, a cat in a hat,
Chasing a butterfly, oh look at that!
The world is a circus, or so it would seem,
With giggles and pratfalls, like a bright, silly dream.

Kites took a tumble, but who could complain?
A pie in the face, just adds to the gain.
The sun painted chuckles upon every face,
As I slipped on a banana, oh, what a grace!

So let's float through this laughter, in joy we will soar,
With a skip and a hop, we'll leave troubles at the door.
In the lightness of being, we'll toss worries away,
And dance like dandelions, come what may!

Visions in the Wind

Sailing through meadows, with thoughts all askew,
A squirrel wearing glasses, oh what could be true?
A voice on the breeze whispered, "Catch me if you can!"
But I tripped on a rock, and there went my plan!

A frog in a bowtie sang tunes of the day,
While butterflies giggled, just dancing away.
Laughter filled the air, like bubbles in a bath,
As I chased after rain clouds, and slipped on my path.

The trees whispered secrets, but I just stood still,
With a pie in my hand, oh what a thrill!
"Eat me!" they chimed, with a wink and a grin,
As I dove for the crust, letting chaos begin.

And as visions in laughter blew softly around,
My heart did a jig, and I jumped off the ground.
With giggles and whimsy, we greeted the day,
In a world full of wonder, we'll frolic and play!

Fractured Stillness

In a garden of chaos, where silence is loud,
A chicken in boots formed a curious crowd.
With a hop and a skip, she punctured the peace,
Bringing laughter and clucks that would never cease.

The sun took a break, lost in a book,
While clouds threw a party, come take a look!
They tossed around marbles, and rain fell like spritz,
While puddles performed, in a weird little skitz.

A toaster was dancing, its bread popping high,
And I couldn't help snorting, while watching it fly.
In fractured stillness, the world felt insane,
As roses debated the value of rain.

So we chuckled together, in moments divine,
As the ants held a meeting on the edge of the line.
In laughter we found all that makes life a thrill,
And danced through the madness, with joy to fulfill!

The Call of the Untamed

A raccoon wore a cape, and a hat made of cheese,
He beckoned the wild with the greatest of ease.
"Come join the parade!" he called with a grin,
As we stumbled on adventures, let the fun begin!

The hedgehogs were raving, or so it appeared,
With disco balls spinning, their passions all cleared.
An owl spun records, while frogs kept the beat,
And I tried to breakdance, but fell on my feet.

The moon, dressed in laughter, looked down from above,
While crickets recited their poems of love.
The call of the untamed was loud in the night,
As we rolled on the grass, filled with pure delight.

Each giggle a spark in the dusk's gentle glow,
Embracing the moments just letting them flow.
In a world wild and wacky, we'd twirl with no fear,
For in laughter, we find that the wild is quite clear!

Whispers of Floating Bloom

A flower took a leap, oh what a sight,
Twirling in the breeze, it danced with delight.
It thought it was a bird, soaring so high,
But landed on a cat, oh me, oh my!

The cat looked up, with a shrug and a sigh,
As petals clung on fur, oh my, oh my!
The flower laughed, saying, 'Let's take a ride!'
And off they went, a curious feline glide.

They tumbled down the street, like a silly dream,
With giggles from the flowers, bursting at the seam.
Every step a giggle, every leap a chat,
That silly, floating bloom, atop the cat!

But soon the games were done, the fun would cease,
As allergies approached—'Oh sneeze, oh sneeze!'
With a puff and a whirl, it bid its farewell,
Leaving cat and flower to their sneeze-filled spell.

Secrets on the Wind

The wind whispered secrets, tickled my ear,
Said: 'Did you know? Flowers can steer!'
They fluffed up their petals and started a race,
But all fell down, right in a muddy place.

A daisy cried, 'No fair! I slipped on a shoe!'
While roses got tangled, oh what a hullabaloo!
Sunflowers just laughed, with heads held up high,
'We're only here for the sun and the pie!'

Then there came a breeze, playing creative tricks,
Lifting lilacs high, making them do flips.
They twirled through the air, a dancing bouquet,
Saying, 'Join us, dear friend, let's frolic today!'

But just as they leapt in joyful parade,
A bee buzzed by, all fun to invade.
The flowers would scatter, all taking their stand,
As secrets were whispered by the bees on command.

Tides of Fragile Beauty

In the garden by the sea, flowers swayed about,
Caught in salty breezes, with a giggle and shout.
Along came a crab, with a swagger so fine,
Said, 'Dance with me, lovelies, let's have a good time!'

The blossoms all trembled, unsure what to do,
But soon they were spinning, colors bright and new.
The crab led the way, with moves like a pro,
While petals flew wildly, in a vibrant flow!

But oh, what a blunder, the crab lost its grip,
And landed in a flower, a surprising trip!
All the locals laughed, a sight blooming free,
A crab in a petal—how silly, you see!

Now legends are told of that whimsical night,
Where flowers and crabs danced under moonlight.
A tide of fragile beauty, so merry and bold,
Turns out fresh blooms can have stories retold!

Lost Fragrance in the Air

A lavender breeze floated right past my nose,
But where was the scent? To my surprise, it goes!
I chased it around, through each nook and cranny,
Only to find it lodged on a fanny!

'Excuse me, dear friend, that's quite the bouquet!'
Said a rose with a wink, joining the play.
'You've got my perfume, return it with haste,
Or else all of us blooms shall smell like a waste!'

A sunflower chimed in, 'Let's all make a fuss,
For a whiff of sweet fragrance, we simply must!'
So they launched into action, forming a band,
Of fragrant crusaders, united they stand!

But alas, the scent slipped, under a bush it lay,
In silence it giggled, having its own day.
So flowers must often learn to share joys,
For even lost fragrances can bring forth the noise!

www.ingramcontent.com/pod-product-compliance
Lightning Source LLC
Chambersburg PA
CBHW071850160426
43209CB00003B/487